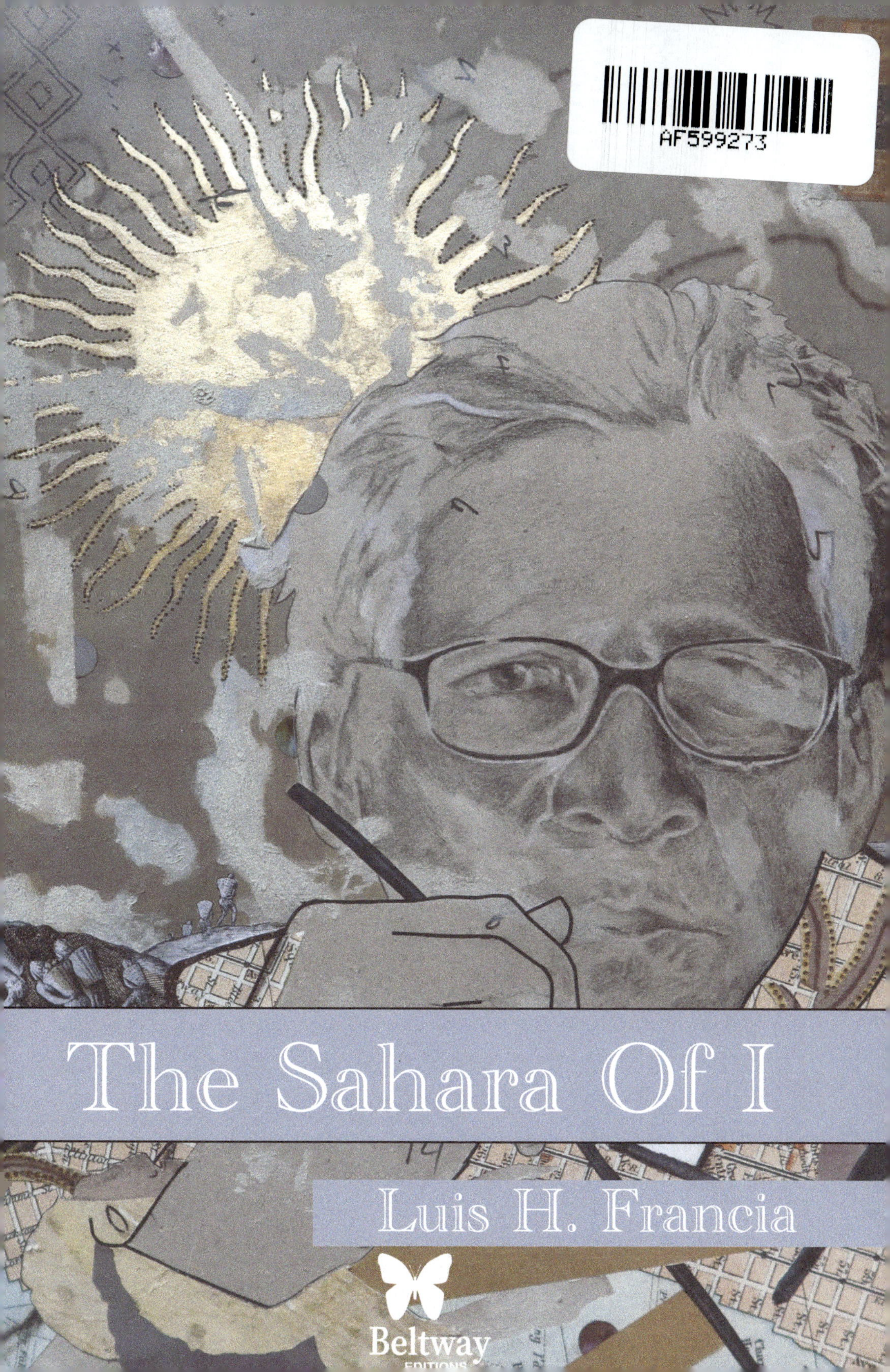

The Sahara Of I

Luis H. Francia

The Sahara of I

Luis H. Francia

Published by Beltway Editions, 4810 Mercury Drive, Rockville, Maryland 20853.

Printed in the United States of America

Cover Art: Kawayan de Guia
Cover Design: Sara Cahill Marron
Author Photo: Midori Yamamura
ISBN: 978-1-957372-09-9

Beltway Editions
www.beltwayeditions.com
4810 Mercury Drive
Rockville, MD 20853

Publishers:
Sara Cahill Marron
Indran Amirthanayagam

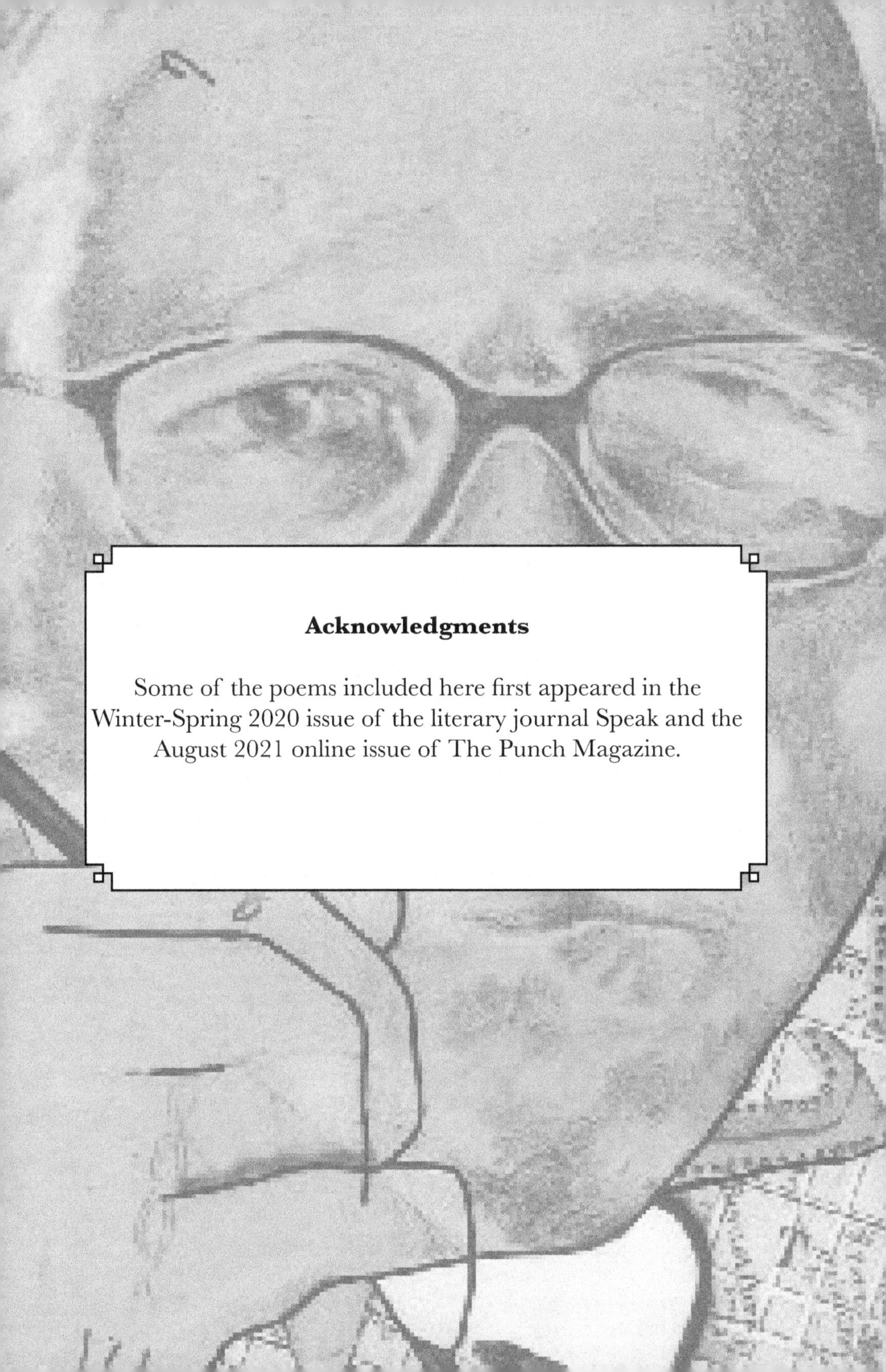

Acknowledgments

Some of the poems included here first appeared in the Winter-Spring 2020 issue of the literary journal Speak and the August 2021 online issue of The Punch Magazine.

Table Of Contents

III.

The Sahara of I

Luis H. Francia

I.

Dia de los Muertos

Because I could not go to the dead
the dead came to me.
Because it was the right day for love
they came with their music, their
oils, their rituals, and their drums.
They walked through my living room and
sang in a multitude of tongues,
in all the languages of the heart.
I laid out bowls of scented water, salt,
bolts of silk, flowers, and my own poems.

They said
remember us for we are
your dead.
They said
when you break bread
leave a piece for the dead.
They said
when you speak, remember
our voices, our songs, our dreams.

They stood around me in a circle
and the circle became me
and I became the circle
on a day that was the right day for love.

Benediction

Blessed be the berserk,
we who kick at the thought of
Earth the sacred ark melting
have not had our fill of singing.
In the precints of hell how will we forgive?

No pity for the gods at the controls,
creators of what exactly, fossil
fuels fueling fossils, a failed
species gnawing at our own feet
to justify rubber on the road?

Why that's highway rubbery, haha.
We'll need no moon to go lunatic.
All we need is more and more plastic!
No privateer's flag to run up, as,
renegades singing, we lop

heads off that tell tall tales one too
many. In the meantime let us
warm ourselves in the brightening of the light
before the sun, once our friend,
now our foe, tells us we're toast.

Time Out

How face down a history of loss?
Which corridor to follow, what
door to go through is unknown.
The past you bear
is not your past,
and the present eyes you
as you would a homeless
stranger who suddenly appears
at your step.

The future eludes you.

There is time that lies
unopened, a Pandora's Box,
or not, it
may contain dead stars,
or a constellation whole and
glorious, or your other lives but
close to disappearing

down the black hole of
oblivion.

Time not looked at
Time not felt or seen
until your eyes
fall upon it.

Bedside, at the Hospital

Halfway out of your body
you take one more look around
this room—I sense this
brief examination, I at your
bedside, unwilling onlooker,
as with others, to your
departure: here now, gone now.
But not yet.

In a weird reversal of flight
the engine of your body shifts into
reverse before the take-off.
You are in this world though
no longer of it, you bid adieu to
one, two, then to all. Everyone
comes to their senses as
you take leave of yours.

Your body finally slumbers.
Now you are wide awake.

Corridors

I.

The way of death begins
the moment we open our mouths.

What good will the sirens do?
The banging on the roofs, the exhortations—
semaphores of a raging grief.

II.

The rabid dogs of fear
run down hospital corridors, down
a wilderness of empty avenues, forever
chewing the bone of pain in a
pandemonium of a pandemic.

What we consume is ourselves.
We must think of better feasts.

III.

The way of death ends
the way it begins,
the mouth open only a
moment, to suck in a
yell, a sigh, memento mori.

IV.

Breathe in the interval,
pursue a song to encompass
all words elusive, to circumscribe
pain with shields, never mind the glory.
Let mind be the mouth,

Be a bird in a serenade, then
burrow beneath days and nights
feathered in silence and love.

Nightmare Assassin

Corona, you are Cain and
worse than Cain.
For you were never my
Brother.

I know you, Agent COVID-19,
master of stealth, nightmare
assassin. You take on other
people's breath, to

Leap into mine, or from
hands unsuspecting, scale
the battlements of my
tell and through the

Windows of my soul, turn
this keep into a castle
of grief! I block and
parry, mask and simple

Soap, my foil. Foiled! Though
you will once more
lay siege, though you may
even make me weep

I will not be your host,
nor your keeper, I only
have this to say: Drop
dead, you creep, you

loveless son of a bitch!

Haiku

Grief is my castle
and there immured I will live
until the reprieve.

Breathe from the Heart

I deal in ideals, not ideologies
I spurn idols and idolatry
my idiom, paradigmatic,
my id, idiosyncratic but not idiotic.
I'd do in an instant the opposite,
abdicate from a realm where the
locksmiths preen, the subjects are a nullity,
the flesh and myself, spirit big
as Idaho, flat as Iowa
I ideate over what I eat and ate
Why not

Breathe from the heart
All else is dust.

Masks

We are in the clear now
and our thoughts sail towards one another.
Let me take you on board, where
love will be the wind
that navigates our ship through
straits Magellan never saw—

a Pacific only you and I know.
In the company of blue fin
In the long-delayed steps we
Take, the hugs we give each other.

We will sing the absence of masks
And cast away the masks of absence.

Views to Chase Away the Lockdown Blues

From our fifth-floor aerie, now cell, I
spot my neighbors clad in fur who pay no
maintenance fees nor assessment charges.
For they are free, free in a tree! Free to
lead such swinging lives, hedonists all,
whether backyard aerialists or speed
demons careening up and down the
leafy highways and their branches.

Sometimes do they engage in quarrels, these
squirrels, or avid courtships where the squire never
takes No for an answer. Birds and the bees leave them
be, and bushy tails tell a tale I will not see behind the

Bushes, allowing them the privacy I no longer have,
their intimacy not to be Instagrammed, Facebook'd,
Twittered, and SnapChatted. But they raise no scandal,
pay no heed to social distancing—au contraire—
commit no mayhem, nor murder,
nor keep me from my night-appointed slumber
nor do they raise a fuss when through my open
window the raucous blast of horn and drum and
piano shakes their leaves. For all I know, they too
have their dens of cool chattering knowingly, over
roasted acorns and beetle juice, of Bird, Miles,
Coltrane, Ella, Louis, and Billie, sharers secret
I salute, in the symphony of this maddened city.

Being with a Bee

He was busy.
Of course.
I was busy.
It was his nature.
It wasn't mine.

I needed to move
there on the roof
and shake off the
quarantine blues.
He, always on the move,
even when still
there on the roof.

He multi-eyed me
a jigsaw puzzle he
knew too well: a human!
Burner of hives, despoiler
of flowers, too often the enemy!

He hovered, not too far
not too near, right at
the border unseen but felt
between him and me.
Fight or flight?

I jogged around the roof
nearing then distancing from
his border, just as he too,
to mimic or mock me
flew in amazing circles, but

never crossing that line.
A treaty of sorts, a truce.
And so I slow and halt

and saw bee doing the same
waiting as though for
my questions.

Have you seen angels?
Do you have favorite flowers?
How high can you fly?
Have you sheltered in place?
Have you grieved lately?

There on the roof he hovered
then zipped and zoomed up
into the blue. I knew he
understood that these
questions were for myself,
my destiny. His was to be bee
and that was enough.

The Cardinal

Red-robed, on his wooden pulpit
opposite my window, he regards
his diocese quietly, noting the
file of squirrels in their brown
habits pausing for prayer,
the secular cat basking in the
pagan sun. Sparrows dip their
wings in reverence.

The wind whispers news of a
conclave. He hurries on to Rome.

New York Anthem

We are bright and brown
black, yellow, red, and white

We stand side by side,
Africans, Asians, Hispanics,
Gentile, Jew, Arab, Native American

Tall and dark
short and fair
thin and sweet
stout and bitter
wizened and the wise
strangers at once and friends

We raise our hands to
show we have no arms

We raise our arms to
dance, to put around
one another, to kiss

We raise our arms and
bid you, come!

All thirst
all are at peace
drinking from
this rainbow-colored oasis
Democracy!

15th of May: Birthday Poem for My Mother

May! the happiest month,
mid-May the happiest of all,
spurning winter's cold hands to welcome
the sun's long-armed embrace.
May! coaxing flowers from the land
that once again reclaims its magic!
May! That brings feasts of mothers
to rival those of royal courts!
Your birthday now, Mother, marks nine decades
in the vineyards, ninety times Earth has gone
full circle, you, tirelessly mothering.
Three sons, two daughters—Henry, Joseph,
Myrna, Luis, and Judy—are the harvest
of a life that has had its lean days,
the too-often scarce apportioning of
luck and bounty, but also its share
of love, blessed if not
with the grace of wealth, then with the
wealth of grace, health, and friendship too.
Music there is to your life, that even now
keeps playing (as you keep playing ivory),
andante, then pianissimo, molto allegro, in sync
with the sacred music of the spheres, matrix
of all movement, as you are matrix of ours.
May! Your ninetieth spring, Mother,
and you still have that swing!
May! May its flowers bloom even more on this day!
May! May the love of your sons and daughters
keep you and the earth turning!

The Good Ship Alice

For Alice H. Francia (1915-2006)

The body is the soul's vessel.
The soul: passenger and
Captain of the ship.

Once I was a voyager on this ship, Alice,
secured by love to a hold
that was my second skin and first city.
Privileged passenger was I on that primal
trip, captive and master at the same time,
kicking up a storm and delighting in
the way my city grew.
When at the voyage's end, I was
disembarked at a port with too bright
lights and harsh sounds, I protested
loudly at my abandonment but
I had been only moved to the
upper deck where now I had a view.

Mother undertook that voyage six
times, with one loss at sea, a later
passenger whose memory will never
be with me. She steered us through
storms, and sailed giddily when
tempests held their breaths and
gracefully when they did not, a
craft as sturdy as she was handsome.
Now she lies drydocked on a hospital
bed, her face still a valentine to
beauty ninety days shy of ninety one.
No amount of repairs will ever right the
mothership again, no matter how skillful

the nurse, how vigilant the sentinels of
IV, the daily sun, and our ministrations.

Life's waters will never see that keel
plunge in again. Run ragged, full of
leaks, now being decommissioned,
Alice is moving on to a different sea
and her sons and daughters are bereft.
Nothing to do except gather about,
prayers and wishes on hand for the
smooth end of a voyage and the
start of a new one.
May the Good Ship Alice that once cradled me sail
smoothly on the new sea, as she does
in the love that fills my heart and memory.

Inversion

To predicates we attribute the strangeness
of nouns, as if by naming we can feel
the sharp space of a mind.
But suppose God concludes,

"I have no plan, so keep
your shirt on in this labyrinth."
We clutch our brains, foreknowledge
spreadeagled but

beyond the swell of paws, and
after remembering
the dark angels of Samarkand—
no sound but the quickening of light—

we worship in a cathedral of
pearl, between a hard place and
the fog. Things teeter, only my
predicates remain: brown, human.

Nouns swoon in uncertainty,
and all we can foretell
even blessed with a fox's head
Is a realm of nought.

II.

La Noche de Federico Garcia Lorca

Under siege, he was indignant
the writer in his lair.
History shook his tray,
upsetting his meal of fact.
The afternoons of Granadan light
should have washed away
the black shirts, should have

laughed in strongest protest.
People knew. His body
quavered just then
as though lightheartedly funny
but it was his queerness trembling
when night arrived, full
of noticing, full of

Them

Men perhaps he might have
loved some other time
at some other place

He turned his pages away from

Them,
Them

filled these with knives
and infamy

Them
feared and fearful

sicced the dogs of darkness on
the home where Bernarda Alba was born
and the dense yo te quiero verde garden
from where Granada's Adam was by

Them
banished forever

New World Caliphs

By the banks of the Euphrates they
have set up their air-conditioned tents.
What is it these new caliphs from the West want?
What revelations, what angels, do they seek
in the desert, with their armor, their guns, and their money?
Do they seek in the sands their
endless god endlessly, for an endless war?
In Baghdad, Nineveh, in
Mosul and Fallujah, in Kabul and
Kandahar, an eternity of gunfire nightly
knocks on every door.
How many lambs will propitiate
their desire for slaughter?

Imagine Alienation

In the king's mind, nostalgia's storyline
escalates to a spectacular with butcher's knives,

and expeditions alter the Native and the Arctic.

In the king's mind, the aged forbear the
telling, the epic length of identity.

Give us this day our daily bread

before the poison of intelligence
melts the polar caps of our

imagination, and all hell

colludes to stretch over us
a silk web of nightmares.

In the king's mind, such is

the topography of empire:
Capital eating climate,

Revolutions eating children.

In the king's mind roses of applause
for women alluring in their repression

and men brave as soldier boys.

We are as lonely as magicians in private.

The Book of My Life

My tongue tastes of too much understanding.
Too many pieties has it uttered.
Too many words roll off, a faucet
that will not shut, dribbling from
my mouth, from everyone's mouth, the
pool of verbiage rising until we drown, still
smiling, in anomie and ennui, and we
stifle our breath with our breath, not
recognizing our own deaths.

What about the prophecies of childhood?
What about the everyday truths with their
little thorns that pierce and cling to us?
Only the bloodless need not worry
for they will not bleed.
This is our daily truce, our fearful covenant:
To keep silent about the aggressions we bear,
about the rocks hidden beneath the polite
phrase, Pharisees that we are, and the nails
we hammer into each other.

I tire of complaints and pleas, and so
abdicate my role and abjure such tongue.
Let the stars come and listen, let the flowers rise to
hear what I say, and the trees hoist me atop their
crowns so I can refresh and astonish the sky.
God pauses, she pauses and she will
take note and surely she will change
the book of my life.

Java Reverie

With the first cup, wolves slink
away before the morning light, back into the
tundras of my brain. I step warily
into a life—my own, a strange role
though I have always played it, several
decades running, often to an empty house.
All the missed cues I know by heart,
all the lines people have come to expect.
When did I audition for this?

Surely there exist better parts!

So I feel on my second cup,
where the rows are packed, an audience
cheers me on as I win against
all odds, tracking down bad
scribes with their works of mass
distraction to school them cold—
a simpler, strong-jawed life
where no qualms but only palms
are brought together in loud praise and

shekels fall as easily as autumn
does at my feet.

I will replace myself and hire another me.
Who will stride onto the stage and be he?
Let him now begin with the third cup.

Cat in the Act

Air has fur,
Fire a face

Water has feet,
Earth a mane—

Craft, the Cat:
Act of pure art!

Feline Groovy

Why do cats up bound,
down plunge with unnatural
ease? Are they fallen angels
bereft of wings, yet the pull of air
remains stronger than earth's?
Are they felons who waltz and tango
through the bars of gravity,
defying divine justice?
Amber, ivory, calico, midnight, and quartz
their tight jumpsuits that
shade them lest we be blinded
by their dazzling flights.
When a feline falls, it falls from
grace into grace.

CatDog

what if miaow refused to cat,
and bark balked at dog,
would the world still go
and moo begin to cow?

what if coo sulked at
dove, rhyme unreasoned?
what if infinity abdicated
from god, and sea retreated
forever from shore?

would my growth still be
to love vaster than vegetable?
would love still be love,
fill me? would I still be I,
love you?

ah, but a miaow always
cats, and bark never balks.
so let me miaow your cat,
and you, bark my dog!

Tiger Mouse

In the morning I am both a
tiger and a mouse,

frightening and
amusing my wife.

Between the roars and the
squeaks, a rooster crows.

I am that, too.

The Acrobat

Consider the Buddha,
Who moves without moving:

First step same as the last,
Last smile same as the first.

Acrobat of great agility!

Wild Garden

I need less divinity and
more humanity to offset the
accidents of my upbringing.
A hound for heaven I am not.
I can cross myself Catholic
fashion with the best of
them, and still scratch my crotch.

Being human is all I want!

I would rather kneel before the altar
of feminine flesh than cold plaster.
No contradiction there, in the
theology of my thinking,
where Peter is in my kind
of heaven, where the portal's
a narrow squeeze, thereafter
a wild garden and I,
gardener gone wild!

Benny the Bedbug Goes to School

Bedbugs found in New York schools—news item

It was a momentous occasion, and I wanted to make Mom and Dad proud. I would be going to school, the first in my family to do so. My parents and my older siblings had all sucked it up so I could lodge in the nooks of a wooden desk at PS 132.

My parents, bless their black little hearts, had worked long and hard under life-threatening conditions to make sure their little Benny had enough food to not miss a day in class. They were pulling for me, and so was my extended clan, out in Bushwick, Astoria, and Chelsea—all different places where while conditions were somewhat rough provided us all with enough warm bodies. It's the old story, like many of the tales we read in Mrs. Ramirez's social history class, you know, the young 'uns rising above the hardships and hardscrabble lives of the previous generation.

Mom and Dad had always dreamed of living a life of luxury, as my distant cousins were at the Waldorf Astoria. They were relations on my mother's side, kind enough but a bit puffed up, if you know what I mean. Uncle Roderick, their paterfamilias, was fond of my dad, and so invited us over one holiday season to spend a couple of nights, at their 25th floor residence.

And so it was that we hitched a ride in the plush, fur-lined interior bag of a certain Louis Vuitton. Funny, though, Louis didn't speak with a French accent, as I thought he would but Nicholas, my older cousin who was attending Dalton Prep, said this would-be Louis was actually a portly gentleman named Jake, traveling with his wife Martha on holiday from London. Middling-class, Nicholas sniffed.

Nicholas had grown up, a bug of privilege, you see. He didn't look too kindly on the nouveau riche, nor on us either, though out of respect and fear of his dad, he held his class contempt in check, and sometimes managed to even be nice. He had drunk, as his parents had, only from the richest blood. Type A, naturally, was their drink of choice, and Bloody Mary was their favorite cocktail. And the succulent blood sausages Aunt Agatha had prepared for us were to die for.

That first night we had quite a feast. The gentleman and his wife who were not Vuittons after all, got so smashed on Champagne that they could not feel our slings and arrows, though from time to time an errant hand would scratch where moments ago some of us had supped. And what a supper! Oysters, chateaubriand, sweetbreads, caviar, very good reds, chocolates, and the aforementioned Champagne, all now coursing through their veins.

Sated, we all slept, as the saying goes, snug as bugs in a rug, ho ho! I had never had such luxurious appointments before. The beddings were unbelievably plush, as were the carpets. In retrospect, writing now as the founder and editor of Benny's Bed & Breakfast (www.Bennysbedandbreakfast.com), those two nights at the Waldorf spoiled me forever. I vowed, once I was on my own, to never again sleep on any bed where the sheets had less than a 1000-thread count. I have never looked back.

As for Uncle Roderick, Aunt Agatha, and cousin Nicholas, they relocated to London, hitching a ride with the couple the day they checked out of the Waldorf. Uncle Roderick had decided to accept a long-standing invitation from their English cousins. Yesterday I received a letter from Nicholas, now a regular contributor to BB & B, telling me about his forthcoming marriage to a lovely English bride, rumored to have close ties to the royal family. In fact, the ceremony will be held at Westminster Abbey, in one of the side chapels, with the reception to follow at Buckingham Palace. Nicholas promises that this would be the wedding of the decade, with fountains of Type A and would I please come with my best photographer.

I can't wait to cover this feast!

Book Tweets

The Inferno: A hell of a read!
Moby Dick: A whale of a work!
Scarlet Letter: Put Hawthorne on your A list!
As I Lay Dying: Bill Faulkner's incredible talent will outlive him!
The Odyssey: Don't leave home without it!
Ulysses: Don't leave home with him!
Middlemarch: Even better in early April!
Sense and Sensibility: Only the proud would be prejudiced against this!
Pride and Prejudice: Has loads of sense and sensibility!
Waiting for Godot: Is it worth the wait? Why should we tell you?
The Magic Mountain: The peak of this author's career!
The Bible: So many books, so little time …
In Search of Lost Time: So many books, so little time …
Madame Bovary: M. Flaubert remains faithful to his promise!
Midnight's Children: The same stroke for different folks!
Gargantua and Pantagruel: A hefty tome for healthy appetites!
Tom Jones: You'll have a hard time keeping up with this one!
The Idiot: An unbelievably smart book!
War and Peace: Leo has his cake and eats it, too!
Crime and Punishment: Fyodor takes the cake—and is forced to eat it!
Portrait of the Artist as a Young Man: Eat your heart out, Dorian Gray!
Atonement: Worth a year of indulgences!
Sentimental Education: I wept over this!
Dracula: A work you can sink your teeth into!
Alice in Wonderland: Alice doesn't live here anymore!
A Catcher in the Rye: Much stronger than A Pitcher with a Bagel!

The Sahara of I

Pen, not a ballpoint no, puts
down in place in a pen of a
page likes, peeves, dreams,
hates, detritus—always new
this old challenge, to

find a person lurking in the
Sahara of I, that one who can
speak differently but unbearably
familiar, emerging out of years
of strangeness, my own

Lawrence of Arabia
to approach this oasis, this
genesis, bearing three gifts
for the Holy Child:
Pen, Paper, Word.

Pen Pen de Sarapen*

My pen can be a pen
or un cuchillo de almacen

It can earn my daily bread
or my daily pain
loaves and loaves, or
crumbs

My pen can be a pane
to open, or close
on what you will never see
again

My pen can be a gun
bring grief to some
be a wizard's wand
bestowing light, mystery

My pen can be everything,
seeding on a sheet
a universe of verse

My pen wounds and heals
raises me as easily
from death as can
plunge me into it.

Hail, pen!
Ink god!
Write my life with
your blood!

**in Manila, a line that begins a nonsensical children's rhyme*

Bar None

Despair demands theater for
such a person as I, for someone
to compile an archive of
notes, to scrawl as I
crawl from bar to bar,
setting it lower
and
lower,
as the drinking gets better
& longer & later.
There I've said it, have
drunk nearly all my
innocence and jewelry,
yet I refuse suicide,
for the main beneficiary
would be me, and I
wouldn't be around to
enjoy it, and so
I hope for another letter,
another note, and most
importantly that stage direction:
Bartender, another whiskey and beer!

Return of the Native

The weather remembers me kindly,
remembers the footfall, smell, and
aura of a man who once lived
here, and puts out a call for a breeze,
and some cooling clouds to protect
me from heat's scolding.

The landscape bears me no rancor on
my absence and too brief return.
What was a dull trek is now a treat.
The sky, subdued,
is in a conciliatory mood.
Sentinels on the beach, palm trees
eye me warily but

let me pass. The South China Sea,
on the other hand, is delighted,
and gambols at my feet, beckoning.
I plunge into it, two long-ago
friends lost in a tight embrace.

A Love Poem in Russian

For M

I wish to utter frippery
in Russian
I wish I could be slippery
in Russian
slug down vodka by
the river Volga
in Russia
converse with the
Lady and her dog
under the trees of
the cherry orchard
in Russia

How does one speak
of war and peace,
court Anna K
if not in Russian?
Let me sing of
St. Petersburg's sky
carouse in Moscow
With that cabaret choir

The Brothers K
crooning about
Crime and Punishment
in Russia
If I get sick as a dog, why
there's always Dr. Zhivago!
Leave Lenin aside and
for god's sake don't bring
Stalin in but push me
my Pushkin, babushka,
and my melancholy Anna Akhmatova
in Russian

Above all a kiss to you
my green meadow, my darling
about whom
I would write love poems
As vast and as wide as
The steppes of
Russia

Debris of Brides

The debris left by brides unwanted,
my verse may not serve well,
nor oil the gear of their rage.
Not even a seminar of marines

In a race can care for them, though on
the road none can match their gung-ho ardor.

All I can do as a sign is sing,
a happy dirge on a far-off ridge,
At once a prayer that my song be a
wand waved, a bridge across
to summon the dawn, a

Morning to cater to
what's at stake rather than skate
around, and bless their unhappiness

That brides disgruntled may forsake
their bridles to leap beyond the
pale and hear the peal of light.

Spring Jig

I.

The small wind moves
as a leopard, cunning on
padded feet, and
leaps upon its quarry:
Paper, dust, and grass.
Whirls them around and around
in cat's play, and up and down
or is it, perhaps, that
paper, dust, grass
for one moment spring
alive, and do a dance
an impromptu ball
announcing to one and all
their brief and lively
Insurrection?

II.

A whorl
          is a
wind with
grecian curls

Thoughts at a Poetry Reading

My skin is blue, not
from the wind on the
corner or the waves
from the sea, but
from the retelling of
the retelling.

This is not brand-new,
this is simply retailing.
More than old hat,
it is very very old hat
pointing to leaves a
thousand times told

Its author a glam no one,
tailor of hand-me-down
hand-me-down tales
that may have been tall once
but no longer: pygmies on sale!
He a likely candidate
for my necktie
party, to which you
are all invited.

III.

Saturday Night at the Wordello

Wild wild Saturday night!

Verbs, loud and rough in their boots,
stomp in, lusting after nouns.
Adverbs long for adjectives, aggressive in
the parlors. In corners sit the doleful wallflowers,
prepositions to whom no one proposes.
How different for the easygoing conjunctions!
They pair readily, unlike prefixes and their
cousins the suffixes, picky as to whom
to attach themselves.

Wild, wild Saturday night!

Metaphors brazenly
mix, modifiers dangle
from the eaves, similes
grin like drunken idiots, and
gerunds are fabulously bi.
And if you're a favored
customer, erudite in
your grammar, sans taint of ain't,
Madame Split Infinitive
may invite you to a private salon where
she orders Mademoiselle Syntax to
doff her gloves and her gown slow
ly, to reveal in all their glory
parts of her speech!

Wild wild Saturday night!
Let's all go down to the wordello!

The Day I Won the Nobel

The phone sang
with the news.
So too did the sun.
All was glorious, glorious:
Excelsis!

Yet cried I,
what took you so long
to place me above all
pretenders to the throne?
All of them—wrong!

Off with their heads!
Think of what was said,
words and words expended.
When all is said and done
I, above the crowd alone

The rest, scribblers, atrabilious
loathers, not lovers, of
the writ that commands
obeisance, makes us more
than flesh and blood: Immortal!

Phone rings again, again! Reveille!
This time bids body out of reverie, out
of bed, to empty itself awake, once
more be the pedestrian and
face the quotidian!

Unable in Elba

To have met Napoleon in defeat, unable in Elba, would we have been friends?
Full of images and mood swings, connoisseur of coq au vin, when he removed boundaries—Marengo, Moscow, Waterloo— he was l'artiste supreme, short man with the biggest beret on the Left Bank, focused always on beginnings, tattooing history's many arms brilliantly.
He was never modest.
He took Europe, he took Egypt, he could have taken Africa, for those who took him in
were themselves taken in, even Josephine.
I would have shaken that hand in his breast pocket, the hand that more than a sword held a golden brush to paint his face on the red earth.

good thief

I steal what I write against a tock.
Against a tick I build a rock but of paper.

I have no quarrel with Time, that confidence
man, and his claim over my brief reign.

So let my lover weep
let the sun relinquish

Its keep, let the waters
bring me down deep and deep

So long as my rock of paper brings rhyme to
unreason, the unseen to the seeing, and I:

good thief

Blue Weather

To the tick of consciousness, a wonder—
quiet, the swoosh, the shrill, the squeal of
daffodils.
As for doubles, there are
earth and pebbles, woods and
bits of stars that wandered here
lonely, snubbed by clouds.

And here is something
broken, something beautiful
to turn heads.
Calyx of stamen, ochre of
leaf. Meaning goes by, we
let it go, and
wander down to the

Underworld, and knowing the Dog,
hop on the ferry and skip the
queue, never losing sight of
the galaxy, the green fields, the
Van Gogh Yellow
that we may return to,
yet the figures of us loitering in the
graveyard: do we recognize

ourselves, fading brushstrokes?
What might the hand and heart do?

Happening is everything, is
everything happening? Time,
high on itself, shrugs off
all betrayals, stays loyal.
Say, dream your dreams, fill
them with milestones of love,
with blue weather and move forward

lying down. Say,

Dream your end, as you would
Dream your beginning

Daydreaming at Night

The sky invents dogs
and citadels.

Matisse before Matisse.

The river a
meditating monk

Li Po and Bāsho wave from the stars:

Sliver of silver in a
mirror moon.

Yangshuo, Guilin, China

Dusk

The sun goes home
So do the clouds
So do the cows
          and the cowherd

So do my words
So will I

The rafts and the helmsmen
have gone, but

The ancient river stays
The ancient river goes

And the sharp hands of
cliffs hold up
Heaven, hold
          down Earth

allowing my dreams to
dance as I sleep

Yangshuo, Guilin, China

Guangzhou Blues

My hive is without
honey, and I am a bee
without a flower.

Guangzhou, China

q & a

Monsoon!
How soon?
Too soon!

Poetry Is a Port

Where vessels of words
dock to be unloaded according
to the needs of the heart.
Or maybe the head, and even
the gut. Choose or not, the
need will overcome you and
you will be driven to knock the
harbor master on the head
and run off with containers chock
full of the bare rocks of
language. Crack these open
for you are a miner out for
minerals that can turn into precious
stones, the contraband with which
we speak, sing, rage, dream,
curse, to utter as we copulate
and fit our necks and heads
for crowns and tiaras, the jewelry for
kingdoms of adamantine tears and pain.

A Proposal Worthy of My Wife, Doctoral Student

Why not make of me your dissertation?
Am I not worthy of major exploration,
tomes (and poems) of investigation?
Here I am ready to be footnoted toe to head:
better take advantage while I'm not dead!
You can interview me in the kitchen,
on the couch, while immersed in
the tub—aye, there's the rub!
That one so close to you you eschew!
So send your camera crew to interview:
My words, well-chosen, will be few.
My life I am sure will pass the test
devised by scholars only the best.
Whatever Said[1] says, or Michel Foucault[2]
or Derrida[3], there'll be little to deride or fault,
all the more reason for you to gloat,
my would-be doc, so come, ferret out
my secrets so dark and hidden.
They won't yield unbidden.
There's a treasure to be had in your bedmate.
Ask, contemplate, write: I'll yet make you great!

---

1. Quite a bit.
2. His exposition on the traditional ditty "Fréré " is unrivalled.
3. See, for instance, his Deconstructing the Working Class (Paris: Egalité Editions, 1987).

Eternal Tango in Paradise

Paradise of the mind
Forever available, Forever lost

The roll of dice in Paradise
will always come up in
your favor, one of the
elect, always a winner,
never a loser.

For God is on your side, and
your luck will never suck.

Even the devils on R&R from
Hell can come and play
though they always lose, and
accuse the House of bias.
They'll chat with the Angel Gabriel,
poker whiz, and the Angel Michael,
blackjack king, reminisce
about the good ol' days
tell of friends down there
all the news that's hot
who's with Satan, who's not

They may talk of a new circle
reserved for the Donald
to stand, naked, while Beezlebub
tells him again and again,
"Loser! You're fired!"

At end of day the fallen angels
tumble down once more from Eden
and its gambling halls, down to Hell.

Over and over and over again

the infernal in the celestial
the celestial in the infernal

the Dance Eternal

Arms for Peace

For Indran Amirthanayagam

I want to jump into everyone's arms
roared the poet Indran Amirthanayagam
ready for the leap though there
Were no arms in evidence.
What is this business about jumping
Into everyone's arms, said I,
more circumspect about my own desire
to jump into everyone's arms and
be embraced far and wide, as a
member of that odd race, poets
beings of frail means but vast need.
What would happen if
everyone jumped into

everyone's arms but chaos!
I remonstrated, as Indran meditated
longingly on the possibilities of
jumping into everyone's arms. His
eyes gleamed. I would have to
disarm everyone, wouldn't I, his voice
smooth as an infant's cheek
confident of his crackerjack
diplomat's charms. And what,
I in a pique persisted, would you
jump into if everyone were
disarmed? I imagined
vast armies of raised arms

hairy, unhairy, scented, sweaty
willing to be jumped into, myself
At the head of the line.
Indran laughed mightily: Disarm! Disarm!
Why, would we not be weapons of peace,
both architects and missiles?

He huffed as he grabbed me by the neck,
pulled me along as we ran and ran
up to the edge of night where
the world had gathered and we
jumped, two lambs
sailing into everyone's heart
Into the very heart of light

Carousel

In a stranger's eyes I see the past.
Every baby born bears what has come before.

Words stand, events pass. Even the new is not.
Surrounded by history, round and round we go. If I didn't love you then
I will love you now.
If you don't loathe me today, you will, tomorrow.

And so round and round we go:
Our story even before it is told is old. They say, all is vanity.
So you may wonder why I write. What choice do I have?

Today I must write and tomorrow—
The devil take tomorrow!

For the Greater Glory of Dog

From the United States of Religion
I revoke my citizenship
and mail my faith back
to Sears and Roebuck

Now I unchurch and baptize myself
pagan unconditional
for the Greater Glory of Dog

Love, how does one catalogue
it, how number devotion?

And anyway a bed is a better altar
upon which to perform acts
of transubstantiation, where I
say, eat, for this is my body,
where she, touching her wound
murmurs, drink, for this is my blood.

O sacrament we have always seen
if this be sin, let me be obscene, obdurate,
absolved of all saintliness!
Preacher I, in the sanctuary of stained sheets
take the gift of tongue to your arms
murmuring prophecies from pulpited thighs
The forever lord keeper of vodka and semen
Archangel inviting you to the garden of no exile.

Here in the city of the faithless faithful
I lift my spiritual leg
to consecrate ground as New Dog
whose bark blesses, whose
bite infects with light—

Apostle of the underground I

baptize all whose gloria's
in transit, in their implacable trespass
upon a pale, toothless heaven

heretic streets for heretic days.

Buildings look kindly now on me
doors flung open, to speak
dogs and Filipinos allowed.

Hail us, full of grass!
Was the lord ever with me
and why bless my womb when
you can heal it?

Gnawing on martyrdom's bone,
Holy Me, Saint Mongrel, Anointed Cur, and
refuse of a certain shore, I sin
with every breath, with
every nail hammered in
now and at the hour of your
Death

snapshot

They are the sky's sweet and
angelic utterances, clouds that
soothe and shade us from the
brash sun that lashes
beach, dries grass

Oh those sweet utterances can
turn bitter and dark, when gods
hide among them, pointing
their fingers of lightning,
mad cylinders of their arms

a sky heavy with
remonstrances, divine
anger and pain. To assuage
their hurt, heaven
sends down cleansing tears

I turn and turn, bathing in
this benediction, uplifted
face and arms outstretched,
a brown boy once again straddling
dark earth and heart awakening

On Behalf of Dragons and Demons

Dragons there are on the corner,
their fire on hold.
Brother, can you spare a dime?
The old guard they seek
employment, castle keeps to
terrorize, princesses to abduct, slush
funds to hoard. Their
scales could use a shine,

breath mints certainly, and a press
agent but these are super bright
days with nowhere to lurk, perhaps
not even in a child's imagination.
In a nation of explainers and experts,
of the worldwide web, who would fund their
forays, their brazen antisocial acts?

Gone the bêtes noire, the
bad boys of yore, along with
witches and ghouls!
Gone the dark deep
down in sleep, blankets no
longer shields, nor dreams
sanctuaries of the beautifully bad.

Gone too are the knights errant on
their steeds in search of good
deeds, and princesses languish in
distress, their tresses in need
of a good rinse.
What benefit ivory towers without
dungeons, what good grace
without folly?

What use my angel sans my devil?

O bring me back those dragons,
My resplendent demons!
Heaven unearned without the fall
Is no heaven at all.

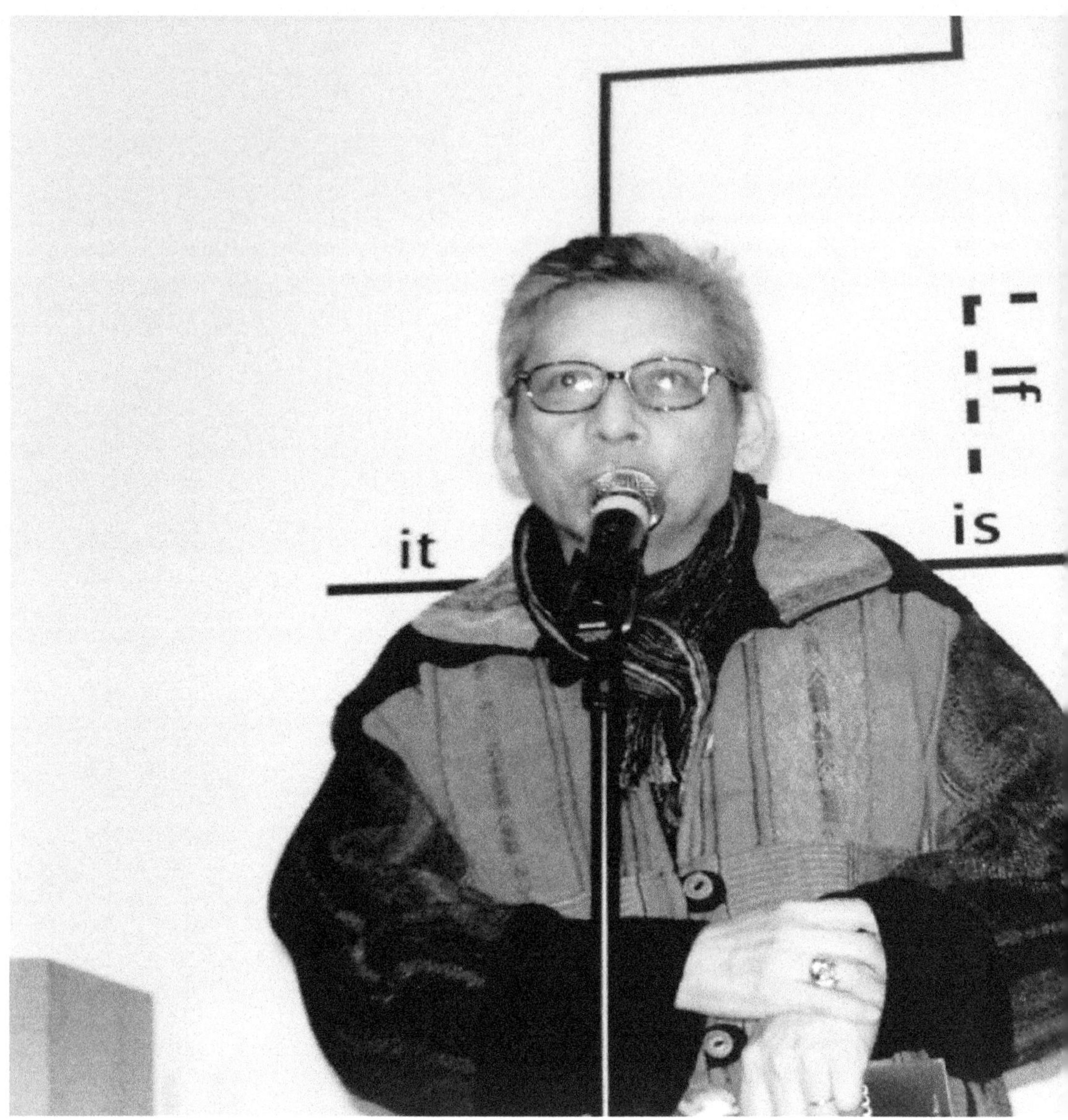

LUIS H. FRANCIA is a poet, playwright, and nonfiction writer. He is an adjunct professor at New York University, where he teaches Filipino Language and Culture.

His last poetry collection was *Thorn Grass* (University of the Philippines Press, 2021). Previous collections include *Tattered Boat*, *The Arctic Archipelago* and *Other Poems*, *Museum of Absences*, and *The Beauty of Ghosts*. Included in many anthologies, he has been a first-prize winner in the Philippines' most prestigious literary competition, the Palancas, and honored by the Union of Philippine Writers in 2014. His works have been translated into Filipino, Chinese, Spanish, French, and German. He has read at numerous literary festivals, including in New York, San Francisco, Chicago, Australia, Canada, China, and Nicaragua.

His nonfiction works include the memoir *Eye of the Fish: A Personal Archipelago*, winner of both the 2002 PEN Open Book Award and the 2002 Asian American Writers award, and *Memories of Overdevelopment: Reviews and Essays of Two Decades*. His *A History of the Philippines: From Indios Bravos to Filipinos* was published in 2010, with a revised edition in 2014. He is in the Library of America's *Becoming Americans: Four Centuries of Immigrant Writing.* His latest collection of nonfiction, *RE: Reflections, Reviews, and Recollections*, was released in 2015.

His first full-length play *The Strange Case of Citizen de la Cruz*, was given its world premiere by Bindlestiff Studio in San Francisco in 2012, and restaged in 2022 by New York's Atlantic Pacific Theater. Another play, *Black Henry*, on Magellan's 1521 landfall in the Philippines, was virtually staged by New York University 's King Juan Carlos Center and Sulo: Philippine Studies Initiative, in late April of 2021, the quincentennial of that historic voyage.

He has taught poetry and nonfiction writing, at among other places, Yale, the Iowa Writers Program, the City University of Hong Kong, Sun Yat Sen University in Guangzhou, China, and St. Benilde College and Ateneo de Manila University in Manila.

He and his wife, Midori Yamamura, an art historian, live in Jackson Heights, Queens.

The Sahara Of I

Printing was completed in July 2024 for Beltway Editions